Experiments
with
PLANTS

Isabel Thomas

heinemann
raintree

Edited by Holly Beaumont and Mandy Robbins
Designed by Steve Mead
Picture research by Jo Miller
Production by Helen McCreath
Originated by Capstone Global Library Ltd
Printed and bound in the USA by Corporate Graphics

19 18 17 16 15
10 9 8 7 6 5 4 3 2 1

Library of Congress Cataloging-in-Publication Data
Thomas, Isabel, 1979- author.
  Experiments with plants / Isabel Thomas.
    pages cm.—(Read and experiment)
  Summary: "Read and Experiment is an engaging series,
introducing children to scientific concepts. Explore the world
of plants with clear text, real-world examples and fun, safe
step-by-step experiments. This book brings botanical science
to life, explaining the concepts and encouraging children to
be hands-on scientists."—Provided by publisher.
  Includes bibliographical references and index.
  ISBN 978-1-4109-7924-7 (hb)—ISBN 978-1-4109-7930-8 (pb)—
ISBN 978-1-4109-7941-4 (ebook) 1. Plants—Experiments—
Juvenile literature. 2. Botany projects—Juvenile literature. 3.
Science projects—Juvenile literature. I. Title.

QK49.T52 2016
580.78—dc23   2014041771

This book has been officially leveled by using the F&P Text
Level Gradient™ Leveling System.

Acknowledgements
We would like to thank the following for permission to repro-
duce photographs: Alamy: incamerastock, 11 (bottom), Martin
Shields, 11 (top), Tim Gainey, 17; Newscom: Flowerphotos Eye
Ubiquitous/Ingrid Michel, 18, G.Cigolono Universal Images
Group/De Agostini, 24, Laura Doss Image Source, 25, Manuel
Cohen Photography, 15, Photoshot/NHPA/Robert Canis, 19;
Shutterstock: Aleksey Stemmer, cover (bottom), ANCH, 7 (as-
paragus), Danny Smythe, 7 (broccoli), Dionisvera, 7 (spinach),
Dmitrij Skorobogatov, 7 (tomatoes), Hurst Photo, 7 (rhubarb),
ILYA AKINSHIN, 7 (lettuce), Maks Narodenko, 7 (carrot),
Ramon L. Farinos, 7 (radish), studio online, 7 (plate), vilax, 6,
wavebreakmedia, 5; SuperStock: Biosphoto, 16

All other photographs were created at Capstone Studio by
Karon Dubke.

We would like to thank Patrick O'Mahony for his invaluable
help in the preparation of this book.

Every effort has been made to contact copyright holders
of material reproduced in this book. Any omissions will be
rectified in subsequent printings if notice is given to the
publisher.

All the internet addresses (URLs) given in this book were valid
at the time of going to press. However, due to the dynamic
nature of the internet, some addresses may have changed, or
sites may have changed or ceased to exist since publication.
While the author and publisher regret any inconvenience this
may cause readers, no responsibility for any such changes can
be accepted by either the author or the publisher.

The publisher and author disclaim, to the maximum extent
possible, all liability for any accidents, injuries, or losses that
may occur as a result of the information or instructions in
this book.

Practical Advice
Mustard, cress, and radish seeds are ideal for the experiments in this book. They are quick-growing and
should germinate indoors at any time of year. Other types of seeds can be substituted, such as peas, bean
seeds, sunflower seeds, or corn kernels, but they will take longer to germinate. Follow the packet instructions.

Safety Instructions for Adult Helper
The experiments in this book should be planned and carried out with adult supervision. Certain steps should
only be carried out by an adult—these are indicated in the text. Always follow the instructions carefully.

Some plants may prick or sting skin. Others are poisonous or can cause allergic reactions even if touched.
Never eat plants that you find growing wild (or parts of plants, such as berries), and always wash your hands
after touching seeds, plants, soil, or gardening equipment.

Remember that it is against the law to dig up any wild plant without permission from the landowner. It is also
illegal to pick flowers in protected areas and many public places. Always ask permission from the owner
before collecting seeds, leaves, fruits, or flowers from a private garden.

Contents

Some words are shown in bold, **like this**. You can find out what they mean by looking in the glossary.

Why Experiment?

What's inside a seed? Why do flowers smell so nice? How does fruit ripen?

Scientists ask questions like these. They work out the answers using **scientific inquiry**—and the really fun part is the **experiments**!

You can be a scientist by asking questions about the world and using experiments to help find the answers.

Follow these steps to work like a scientist:

Ask a question.

Come up with an idea to test.

Plan an experiment.

What will you change? What will you keep the same? What will you measure?

Make a **prediction**.

Observe carefully.

Work out what the results mean.

Answer the question!

An experiment is a test that has been carefully planned to answer a question.

The experiments in this book will help you to understand how plants grow and **reproduce**.

IS IT A FAIR TEST?

Most experiments involve changing something to see what happens. Make sure you only change one **variable** at a time. Then you will know that the variable you are testing is what made the difference. This is called a fair test.

WARNING! Ask an adult to help you plan and carry out each experiment. Follow the instructions carefully. Look out for these signs.

ADULT HELP

Get your eyes, nose, and hands ready! You'll need to observe your experiments carefully and record what you see, smell, and feel.

How Do Plants Work?

Like all living things, plants move, take in food, grow, and **reproduce** (make copies of themselves). The different parts of a plant work together to get these jobs done.

Parts of a Plant

A tiny daisy and a huge oak tree have lots in common. Like most plants, they are made up of roots, stems, leaves, and flowers.

Flowers are where the seeds are made. Each seed can grow into a new plant.

Leaves make food for the plant, using water, air, and sunlight.

The stem (or trunk) holds the flowers and leaves in the right place. It helps the plant move toward the light, and carries water, nutrients, and food around the plant.

Roots anchor a plant in the soil, so it isn't blown over or washed away. Roots also take in water and **minerals** that the plant needs to grow.

Scientists study plants to help people use them in different ways. Plants are a source of fuel, shelter, clothes, and medicines, as well as all our food.

flowers and fruit

leaves

roots

stems

⚠ Many plants (or parts of plants) are not safe to eat. For example, although we eat tomatoes and rhubarb stems, the leaves of these plants are poisonous.

Try to trick a plant

In the right conditions, a seed starts to grow into a new plant. This is called **germination**. A tiny root grows down, and a tiny shoot grows up. How does the seed know which way is up, and is it possible to trick a plant?

Equipment

ADULT HELP

- Seeds (bean, mustard, or cress)
- Cotton balls
- Two glass jars with lids
- Pair of socks
- Water

Method

1 Fill each sock with cotton balls, and stuff a sock into each jar. Add enough water to soak the cotton balls.

 WARNING! Remember to wash your hands after handling seeds.

If you are using bean seeds, soak them in water overnight.

2 Push three to five seeds or beans between the sock and the glass of each jar. Space them out evenly. Put the lids on the jars, and mark them A and B. Put the jars in a warm, light place.

Predict: Which direction will the roots in each jar grow in?

3 Check the jars every day. Make sure the cotton balls stay damp. When the seeds germinate, write down what you see.

4 When the roots are ½–¾ inches (1–2 centimeters) long, turn jar B upside down.

Predict: Which direction will the roots in each jar grow in now?

5 Keep checking the jars every day. Write down what you see. Were your predictions right?

Conclusion

Roots grow down, where they are most likely to find soil, water, and **minerals**. Stems grow up, where they are most likely to find sunlight. When the seeds were turned upside down, the roots and stems changed course, so they were still growing in the right direction. You cannot trick a plant!

What Do Plants Need to Grow?

Like all living things, plants need food to grow. Green plants can make their own food, using water, air, and sunlight.

Sucking Up Water

Plants suck up water through their roots. The water travels up to every part of the plant, through the stem.

SEE THE SCIENCE ↴

Stand some Chinese cabbage leaves in cups of water mixed with food coloring. Put them in a warm, sunny place and watch how the food coloring is sucked up through the plant. You could use this trick to make a bunch of flowers in the colors of a flag or football team!

Taking In Light

Green plants can capture the **energy** in sunlight. They use this energy to make food in their leaves. The food is carried to the rest of the plant. Some of it is stored. Some of it is used as the plant grows.

Plants cannot get up and walk to a sunnier spot, but they can move toward the light. Look at a plant, and you'll see that the leaves are arranged to capture as much sunlight as possible.

Plants also need minerals to stay healthy. They usually find these in the soil and take them in through their roots. The **fertilizers** that farmers and gardeners add to soil are not food—they are minerals to help the plants grow.

Turn Out the Light

What happens to a plant if you take away something it needs? This **experiment** will help you to find out.

Equipment

- Alfalfa, cress, or mustard seeds
- Three empty margarine tubs
- Cotton balls
- Water
- Sheet of clear plastic wrap
- Sheet of wax paper
- Sheet of cardboard

1 Ask an adult to help you pierce six small holes near the top of each plastic tub. This will help air get in when you cover the tubs.

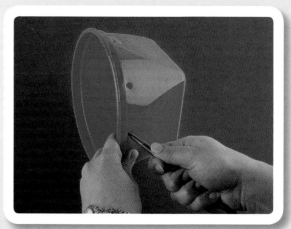

2 Line each tub with cotton balls, and soak them with water. Put 20 seeds into each tub. Put the tubs in a warm, light place, and keep the cotton balls damp.

☑ IS IT A FAIR TEST?

The spacing of the seeds and the amount of water and light should be the same for each group of seeds. How could you make your experiment more fair?

3 After three days, measure the **average** height of the plants in each tub. Record your **observations**.

Find the average height of the plants in a tub by measuring five stems, adding the figures together, and dividing by five.

4 The variable that you will change in this experiment is the amount of light. Place a different sheet of material over each tub. The **transparent** plastic will let in lots of light. The **translucent** wax paper will let in some light. The **opaque** cardboard will not let light in. Leave the tubs covered for two days.

Predict: In which tub will the plants grow best? In which tub will they grow worst?

EXPERIMENT 2

5 After two days, take the covers off the tubs. Measure the **average** height of the plants in each tub, and record your **observations** in a table, like the one below.

	Average height before tubs are covered	Average height after two days covered	Average height after four days covered	Number of leaves after two days uncovered
Tub 1				
Tub 2				
Tub 3				

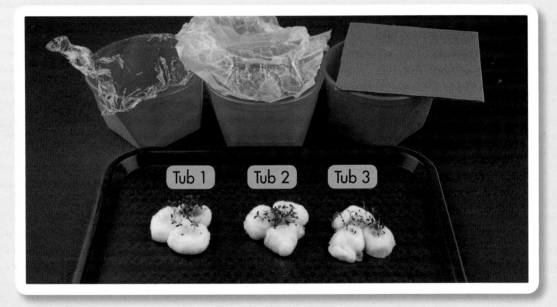

Tub 1 Tub 2 Tub 3

6 Add water, replace the covers, and leave the tubs for two more days. Record your observations.

Tub 1

Tub 2

Tub 3

7 **Analyze** your results. Do they match your predictions?

Conclusion

Did you find that the seedlings with less light grew more quickly? They used the food stored in the seed to grow as tall as possible. They were trying to reach sunlight, which they need to make food. Seedlings with plenty of light grow slower and are stronger.

If you take away something a plant needs, it cannot grow properly. When the plants without light have used up their stored food, they will stop growing and die.

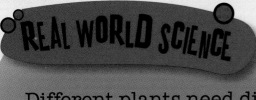

Different plants need different amounts of light, warmth, and water to stay healthy. They are suited to the conditions in their **habitat**. Farmers and gardeners use greenhouses to recreate the habitat of tropical plants.

How Do Plants Reproduce?

All living things make copies of themselves. This is called **reproduction**. Most plants reproduce by making seeds, which grow into new plants.

Seeds are made inside flowers. Each flower has long tubes called stamens, which make powdery pollen. It also has a carpel, where eggs are made.

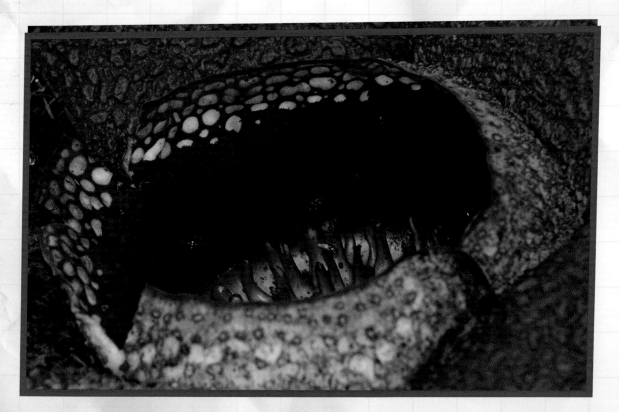

Each flower has colors and smells that attract the right kind of insects. Rafflesia __ers in Asia look and smell like rotting meat, so bluebottle flies pay them a __ __ithout insects, these flowers could not reproduce and would die out.

To make a seed, pollen has to get from the stamen of one flower to the carpel of another flower. This is called **pollination**.

Some plants are pollinated by the wind. They release huge amounts of pollen into the air to make sure that some finds its way to the right place. This type of pollen is the main cause of hayfever, or seasonal allergies.

Plants can't carry pollen from place to place, but animals can. Flowers make a sweet juice called nectar. When insects or birds visit flowers to drink nectar some pollen rubs off onto their bodies. They carry the pollen to the next flowers they visit.

How Does a Plant Spread Its Seeds?

When a grain of pollen joins with an egg, the egg begins to grow into a seed. When the flower dies, it leaves behind a fruit with seeds.

Each seed can grow into a new plant. But if the seeds just fell onto the ground and started growing next to the parent plant, they would have to compete with each other for light, water, and nutrients. To stop **overcrowding**, the plant needs to scatter its seeds as far as possible.

Some plants have fruits that explode to scatter seeds.

Animal Helpers

Some plants grow tasty fruit, berries, or nuts. Animals pick or eat the fruit and move on. The seeds are dropped, plopped, or buried in a different place.

Some plants grow burrs covered with tiny hooks. They cling to the fur of passing animals. They only drop off when the animal stops to clean its fur.

An engineer invented Velcro after picking burrs off his dog's feet and looking at them under a microscope. Velcro has two sides—one with tiny hooks and the other made of fuzzy fabric for the hooks to cling to.

Taking Flight

Many seeds are carried away by the wind. Each tiny dandelion fruit has a fluffy parachute that helps it float in the wind. Others fruits have papery wings, so they travel farther as they flutter to the ground.

Banana races

Unripe fruit is often green, hard, and sour. As it ripens, it becomes sweeter, softer, and may start to smell yummy. These changes help to make sure that animals eat the fruit only when the seeds are fully grown.

What makes fruit ripen? Is it something in the air, or something inside the fruit itself? These **experiments** will help you to find out.

Race 1 – All in the Bag?

1 Pick three green bananas from the same bunch, being careful not to damage the peelings. Put each banana into a different container:
   - A plastic food bag with holes punched in it (use a hole punch)
   - A sealed plastic food bag
   - No container

Equipment

- Bunch of green bananas
- Two plastic food bags
- Marker

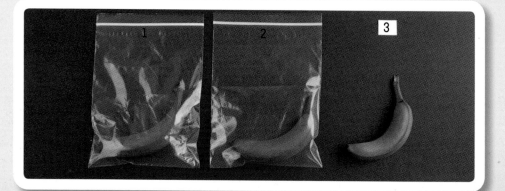

2 Put the bananas in the same room, spreading them out as much as possible. Leave them for four days.

Predict: Which banana will ripen first? Which will ripen last? Write down your predicted order.

3 After four days, how does each banana look, smell, and feel? Look for signs of ripening, such as yellow skin and brown spots. Put them in order of ripeness.

✓ IS IT A FAIR TEST?

Make sure you use bananas from the same bunch, and avoid any that have bruises or broken skin. Change only the container—the temperature, light, and closeness to other fruit should stay the same.

4 **Analyze** your results. Do they match your predictions?

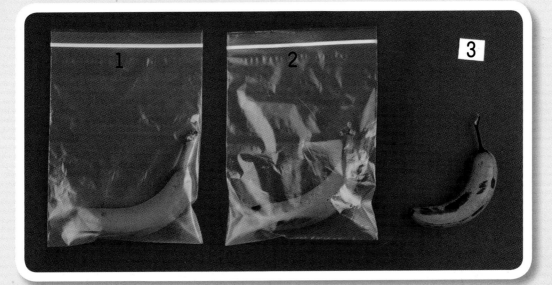

Banana Races

Race 2 – Teamwork

Equipment

- Two green bananas from the same bunch
- One ripe apple
- Two plastic food bags with holes punched in them

Method

1 Put one green banana in each food bag. Add the apple to one of the bags. Close the bags.

2 Place the bags in the same room (but not too close to each other), and leave them for four days.

Predict: Will the green bananas both ripen at the same rate?

3 Look at the bananas in each bag. Look for signs of ripening, such as yellow skin and brown spots. Do the results match your prediction?

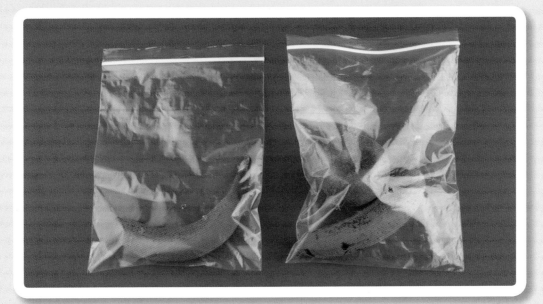

Conclusion

Did you find that the bananas ripened at different rates? Fruit needs **oxygen** from the air to ripen. Once the oxygen in the sealed bag has been used up, the banana cannot keep ripening.

The banana with no packaging had plenty of air, but ripened more slowly than the banana in the bag with holes. This shows something else is involved. As fruit ripens, it gives off gas called ethylene (say "eh-th-leen"). This gas helps the fruit ripen even faster. Keeping fruit in a bag traps the ethylene and helps it ripen more quickly. Holes in the bag let oxygen flow in and out to allow ripening to happen.

The second **experiment** shows how powerful the effect of ethylene can be. Ripe apples give off a lot of ethylene. This helped the green banana ripen more quickly.

How Else Are New Plants Made?

Some plants have special ways to **reproduce**, without making seeds. Part of the parent plant breaks off and grows into a new plant.

Runners

This spider plant has grown a runner with a baby plant at the end. The long runner grows out sideways. When it touches the ground, it grows roots.

Tubers and Bulbs

Some plants store food in bulbs or tubers underground. These are like swollen pieces of stem. If the conditions are right, the tuber or bulb can start to grow new leaves.

Cuttings

Many plants can grow new plants from stems or leaves broken off by animals. Farmers and gardeners use this to grow new plants from stem and root cuttings.

SEE THE SCIENCE ⬇

Cut a 2-inch (5-cm) stem tip from a plant, just below the place where a leaf joins the stem. Remove the lower leaves, but leave one or two leaves at the top. Push the stem into a pot of compost, and keep the cutting watered. You could try growing a seed from the same type of plant at the same time. Which one produces new roots and stems first?

Exact Copies

Plants that grow from cuttings, runners, bulbs, or tubers have only one parent. They are exactly the same as the parent plant. Plants that grow from seeds have two parents. The new plants are different from the parent plants, just as you are different from your parents.

Go On a Sock Safari

Collect seeds with fluffy "animal" feet, and compare the plants growing in different areas.

Equipment

- Two pairs of old adult socks
- Two aluminum seed trays
- Potting compost
- Trowel
- Water
- Plastic wrap

Method

1. Choose two local **habitats** where plants are growing, such as a wooded area, lawn, park, or meadow. Turn the socks inside out and put them on over your shoes. Then go for a walk in each habitat. The best time to do this is early fall, when fruits are ripening. After each walk, take the socks off. Keep them in separate bags until you are ready for step 2.

WARNING!
Take an adult with you on your sock safari.

ADULT HELP

2 Line each tray with compost, and sprinkle with water.

IS IT A FAIR TEST?

Use fresh potting compost. If you use soil from a garden, it might already have seeds in it!

3 Take the socks from the first bag, and carefully cut the ankles off. Place the socks into one of the trays with the soles facing upwards. Cover the socks with a ½-inch (1-cm) layer of compost.

4 Repeat step 3 using the second tray to plant the second pair of socks. Water each tray. Cover the trays with plastic wrap, and put them in a light, warm place. Water the trays every day.

5 When seedlings start to appear, write down what you **observe**.

Conclusion

The fluffy socks picked up seeds from each habitat. These seeds are most likely to be scattered by plants living nearby. If you walked through two very different habitats, the plants that grow in each tray are likely to be different, too. Take a trip back to each habitat, and see if you can match the seedlings to the parent plants.

Plan Your Next Experiment

Experiments have helped you discover some amazing things about plants. Just like you, scientists carry out experiments to answer questions and test ideas. Each experiment is planned carefully to make it a fair test.

Scientists are finding out new facts all the time. Experiments also lead to new questions!

Did you think of more questions about plants? Can you plan new experiments to help answer them?

Being a scientist and carrying out experiments is exciting. What will you discover next?

YOU FOUND OUT THAT...

⬇

Roots always grow down and stems always grow up. A plant can move in a different direction if conditions change.

If a plant does not have light, it cannot make food. The leaves turn yellow and the plant eventually dies.

To ripen, fruit needs **oxygen** from the air. Ripening fruit gives off a gas called ethylene. This can make fruit ripen faster.

Seeds can be picked up by animals and carried far from a parent plant. Even if they are grown in a different place, the seeds still look like the parent plants.

WHAT NEXT?

⬇

Plan an experiment to prove that roots grow downwards because of gravity.

Hint: Try germinating seeds in the dark!

Repeat Experiment 2, changing different variables to find out how they affect growing plants. Try changing the material the seeds grow in, the amount of water, and the temperature. Remember to change just one variable at a time.

Plan an experiment to find out how temperature, light, or damaged skin affects ripening.

Plan an experiment to find out how **overcrowding** affects the way seedlings grow.

Glossary

analyze examine something experiment carefully in order to explain what happened

average typical number in a set of numbers; can be worked out by adding the numbers together and dividing by the number of values added up

energy ability to make something happen

experiment procedure carried out to test an idea or answer a question

fertilizer something added to soil to help plants grow

germination when a seed starts to grow into a new plant

habitat place where a plant or animal normally lives

mineral substance that is found naturally, for example in the soil

observation noting or measuring what you see, hear, smell, or feel

opaque does not let light pass through

overcrowding when too many plants or animals are living in one place, and each one cannot get enough of the things it needs to live and grow

oxygen gas in the air needed by all living things

pollinate move pollen from one flower to another

prediction best guess or estimate of what will happen, based on what you already know

reproduce produce offspring (baby plants or animals)

scientific inquiry method used by scientists to answer questions about the world

translucent lets some light pass through but not enough to see clearly through it

transparent lets light pass through; see-through

variable something that can be changed during an experiment

Find Out More

Books

Green, Jen. *Projects With Plants*. Make and Learn. New York: PowerKids Press, 2015.

Higgins, Nadia. *Experiment With Parts of a Plant*. Plant Experiments. Minneapolis, Minn.: Lerner Publications, 2015.

Waldron, Melanie. *Plants*. Essential Life Science. Chicago: Heinemann Library, 2014.

Websites

FactHound offers a safe, fun way to find Internet sites related to this book. All of the sites on FactHound have been researched by our staff.

Here's all you do:

Visit *www.facthound.com*

Type in this code: 9781410979247

Index